Mel Bay Presents

IRISH HARP MUSIC

Traditional and Original Irish Airs Arranged for Harp, Guitar and Solo Instrument

Arranged by Dennis Doyle

D1528555

Visit us on the Web at www.melbay.com — E-mail us at email@melbay.com

Preface

With the exception of *Austin's Planxty* and *Peace,* which are original pieces, most of the tunes in this book are traditional pieces taken and adapted from the collections of Francis O'Neill, Edward Bunting, Donal O'Sullivan (Carolan material), Manus O'Baoill and Sean Og O'Baoill (Irish-Gaelic airs). The trouble with most of these collections is that there is usually no accompaniment, and if there is any, especially in the case of the Bunting tunes, the arrangement is impossible to play on the non-pedal harp. My task in this book has been to find musically pleasing and comfortable arrangements for these lovely tunes so that they may be played on the folk harp.

The steps that I've taken to prepare these pieces are the same steps that I think anyone could use to prepare a piece for performance. Here are some suggestions about how you might approach traditional material:

• **Listen to traditional players** in sessions and on recordings. Any particular written down version of a piece is just an approximation of the tune, of which there are likely to be many versions. The performer of traditional music is also the composer as she/he interprets the original material, adding ornaments, changing keys or modes, rearranging the parts of the pieces, and filtering the work through her/his own experience and musicianship. Make the tune your own.

• **Play it at the right speed.** If it is dance music, know how fast a reel, jig, slip-jig or hornpipe should be played. The music was meant to accompany dancing. Often we play the music too fast in order to showcase our musicianship at the expense of losing its connection to real people jumping and leaping to the rhythm. If the tune is an air, it's good to be familiar with the actual words of the song, even if it is in Irish, so that you have a sense of the phrasing and speed. If you know the story of the air, your playing should convey the emotional feel (irony, pleasure, sadness, love, regret) of the piece, even if the words are not sung in performance.

• **Proper ornamentation.** It's a poor performance of Celtic music that is played straight through with little regard to proper ornamentation. Again, listen to traditional players. Master the ornaments which can be done on your instrument and exploit the effects that can only be done on the harp. Harpists can do rolls, trills, grace notes, thumb slides, in addition to interesting chord effects and glissandi. Rarely are attempts to note-down ornaments successful. Trust your ear and add them where you see fit. Let your instrument tell you, by how the tune feels on the strings and how the tune is phrased what ornament to use and when to use it. Don't insert it every time the same phrase comes up. Traditional players often change the way they play a tune each time they play it, depending on their mood, whether they are playing solo or with a group, and what the general level of interest, excitement, and communication is in the session. They just sense when the time is right instinctively. A gliss at just the right time, and not overused, often makes a harpist a very welcome performer.

When preparing a tune from scratch, here are a couple things to keep in mind:

• **Melody** - Make sure that the main melody is king. Harpists have a tendency to obscure the tune with lovely harpy arpeggios and busy left hand. Keep it simple.

• **Chords** - When creating chords for the left hand, avoid muddy first-third-fifth (1-3-5) combinations, i.e. chords in root position. For example, playing a C chord by plucking C-E-G within the same octave. Space the notes 1-5-1 or 1-5-3 to give more breathing room in your arrangement. Vary the type of chords and when you use them, leave some silent space here and there.

• **Performance** - Keeping all the above in mind, one should realize that performance is "show business." Modern pop songs are often built upon a clear catchy simple melodic hook. In traditional music, you can find or create a hook based on the tune and use it as the introduction or in the space between the verses. It helps set up and accent the main tune. I also think it is important to give the audience a little story about the tune to help them understand the content of the piece. Doing this helps make the piece memorable and increases the listening pleasure of the audience.

-Dennis Doyle
January 1, 1998

About Dennis Doyle

Dennis Doyle is a Celtic harpist, singer and storyteller. He has done considerable research into his Irish culture, learned the Gaelic language and sings it with love and pride. He has played in Ireland, Japan and throughout North America at most major Irish and Celtic festivals in the last 17 years. He has performed several times on national television, including the show, Murder, She Wrote, and has consulted and performed background music for many others. Dennis and Paula Doyle, along with their children -Evan, Michael, Austin, Grace Bridget and Sarah Kathleen-live in southern California.

Irish Harp Music

from *Hibernia* and the *The Minstrel Boy* recordings
arranged by Dennis Doyle for the folk harp

Table of Contents

Companion music book for the recordings
Hibernia and *The Minstrel Boy* with Dennis Doyle
Cassettes or a compact disk of this music is available through

Incarnation Music
PO Box 1061, Glendale, CA 91209-1061
818-956-1311

ddoyle @ glendale.cc.ca.us

For my son, Austin Dennis Doyle, born on August 10, 1988 in Glendale, CA

Austin's Planxty

Arr. Mark Romano and Dennis Doyle

© 1990

Baltiorum

Traditional Slip Jig

Arr. Dennis Doyle
© 1993

Bishop John Hart *(Sean O'Hairt)* is another tune by Carolan which celebrates the warmth, generosity and tenderheartedness of this man. Although I have listed Hart as a bishop in the title, it is evident from the text that John had not yet been selected a bishop when the tune was written. Of this man, Carolan said: If I were in Rome, as I would like to be, and if they would hear my vote, indeed, I would make you a bishop.

This tune was written during the time of the Penal Laws when a Catholic was not legally permitted to hold title to valuable property. To get around this, many Catholics signed their land over to a trusted Protestant neighbor who held the property in name only. John Hart, and his brother, did just that. They turned their land over to a man named Betteridge, but he was a bad neighbor and simply took the land for his own use, asserting a legal claim, if not a moral one. The laws were so unjust that the Harts had no way to get their land back. Another Protestant neighbor, hearing of this injustice, took the brothers in and gave them part of his property on which to live.

Bishop John Hart

First part without giga

Carolan *Sean O'Hairt*
Arr. Dennis Doyle
© 1990

7

Carolan's Welcome

Attributed to Carolan
Arr. Dennis Doyle
© 1990

Carolan's Welcome is believed to have been written by
Carolan, but the name of the person to whom it was dedicated
has been lost.

The Burnt Out Ol' Fellow

Trad. Irish song *A Seanduine*
Arr. Dennis Doyle
© 1995

Carrickfergus

Traditional
Arr. Dennis Doyle
© 1995

Languid, but with movement

Dark Molly of the Glen

Moll Dubh A' Ghleanna, Trad. Irish
Arr. Mark Romano and Dennis Doyle
© 1990

Dark Molly of the Glen *(Moll Dubh A'Ghleanna)* is one of the beautiful Gaelic love songs. The original chorus says:

She is Dark Molly of the Glen, Dark Molly of the Spring,
Dark Molly, glowing like a rose.
If I myself had the choice of fine young women the world over,
I would prefer my Dark Molly of the Glen.

The Dark, Plaintive Youth

Attributed to Turlough O'Carolan
Arr. Dennis Doyle
© 1995

14

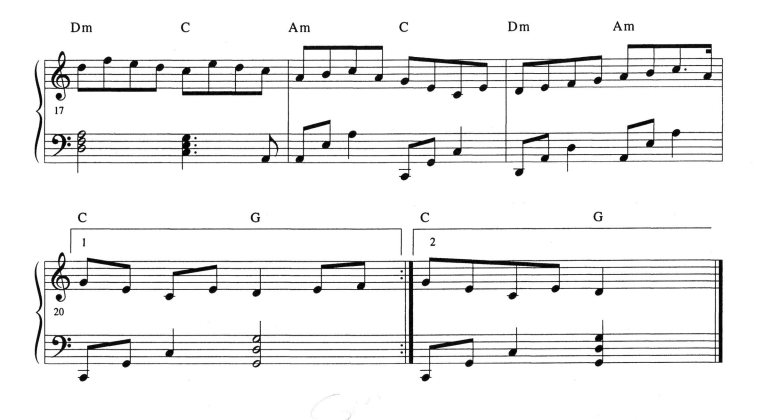

The Coulin (Youth of Flowing Locks), in Irish, An *Chúilfhionn,* dates back to the 13th century when a law was passed which forbade the English in Ireland from wearing their hair in the style of the Irish, i.e. in a *chúilfhionn,* with the front part of the head shaved and with the back part permitted to grow long. Apparently, the English living in Ireland had a tendency to "go native", marry Irish women, and adopt local customs. Before you knew it, they had become "more Irish than the Irish."

The story goes that some bard who lived at the time, wrote this piece in protest, telling the story of a young lady who prefers men who wear the Coulin or *chúilfhionn* hair style. A more modern version uses the image of the Coulin as a young lady. There are Irish Gaelic words to this melody, which, translated, say:

> *Have you see the Coulin? She is by the side of the waves.*
> *Gold rings are on her fingers as she untangles her hair.*
> *It is said that the Pharaoh who governs the ship*
> *Would prefer to have her himself than have Ireland without division.*
>
> *Have you see the dream woman? She is walking on the roads.*
> *The bright dewy morning, not a speck on her shoes.*
> *It's many the green-eyed young man who are looking to marry her,*
> *But they will not get my darling in the way they'd like.*
>
> *Have you seen my young lady this fine day?*
> *She is by herself, her head full of curls falling down to her shoulder blades.*
> *Sweet the young woman and a fine rose on her brow.*
> *Proably each young rake wishes he could have her.*

15

The Coulin

Trad. Irish melody from *An Chúilfhuinn*
Arr. Dennis Doyle
© 1990

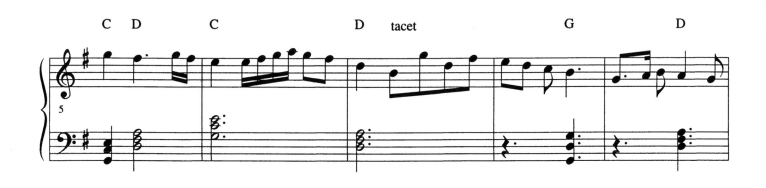

Isabella Burke

Trad. melody attr. to Turlough O'Carolan
Arr. Dennis Doyle
© 1995

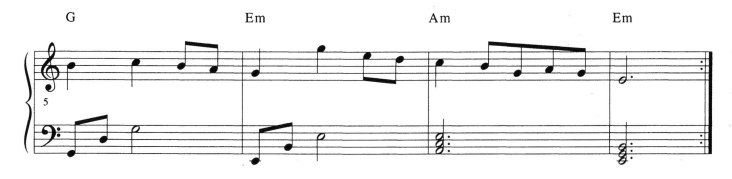

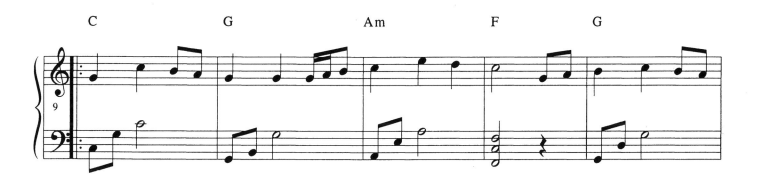

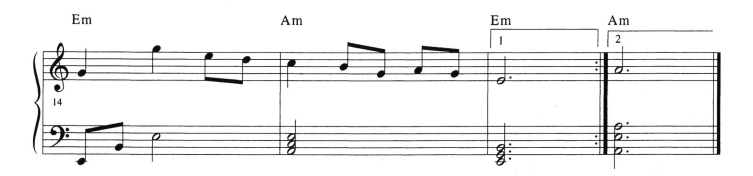

The Fairy's Hornpipe

Trad. Irish from the O'Neill collection
Arr. Dennis Doyleand Mark Romano
© 1990

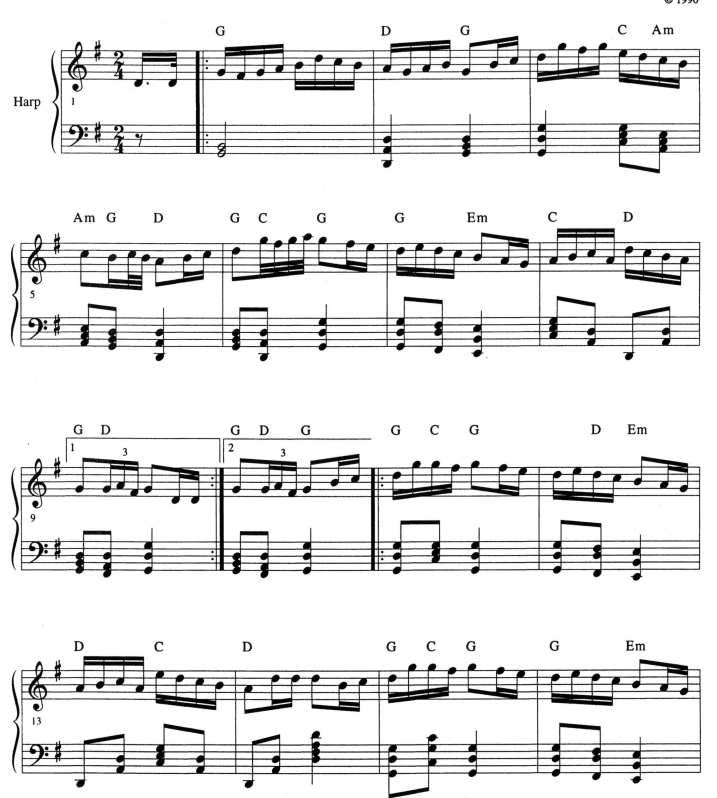

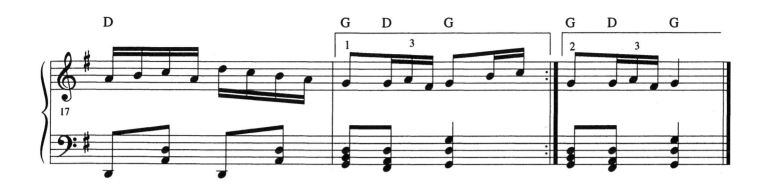

Down By the Beach , *Thios Cois Na Trá,* is a song of sad love. The part I love about this song is where he calls her his "Sun-Treasure." Imagine that!

Down by the beach, there lives my love,
Bright and fair is she, the pick of fine women.
She is a star without blemish, who never lost her blossom.
I read in the Irish language the accomplishments of the woman.

I would get a plentiful store of silk and satin.
Rings would be on her fingers and fine pearls and gold.
I don't want to have business with any but you, Sun-Treasure,
And may I walk the length of Ireland with you and on down to Rome.

Down By the Beach

Trad. Irish, *Thios Cois na Trá*
Arr. Mark Romano and Dennis Doyle
© 1990

The Eirne Boy

Trad. Irish, *Buachaill 'On Eirne*
Arr. Dennis Doyle
© 1993

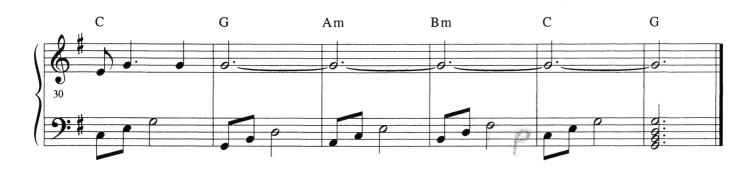

The Eirne Boy, *Buachaill 'On Eirne,* is the source for the modern song entitled, **Come By the Hills**. It remains a most beautiful love song in either language. Here is the translation of part of the original Irish:

> *I'm an Eirne boy and I'm looking for a nice young girl for myself.*
> *I wouldn't need a dowry for her. I am rich enough already.*
> *The measure of Cork is mine, both sides of the valley, as well as Tyrone,*
> *And unless things change, I am heir to County Mayo as well.*

> *I am not accustomed to herding cows or any of that,*
> *But to playing and drinking with nice young women on the mountain.*
> *If I lost my Darling Treasure, it's likely that I would lose my reason,*
> *Your kiss is greater in worth to me that the use of a shoe for a year.*

Give Me Your Hand

Trad. Irish, *Tabhair Dom do Lámh,* attrib. to Rory Dall O'Cathain
Arr. Dennis Doyle
© 1990

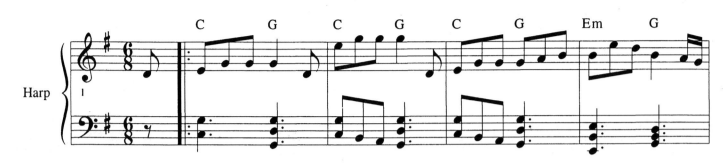

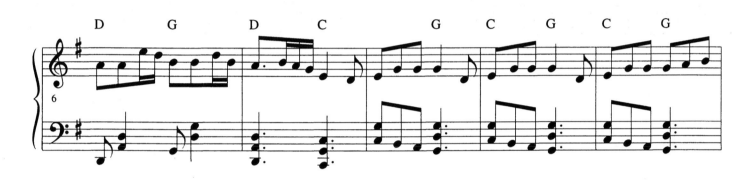

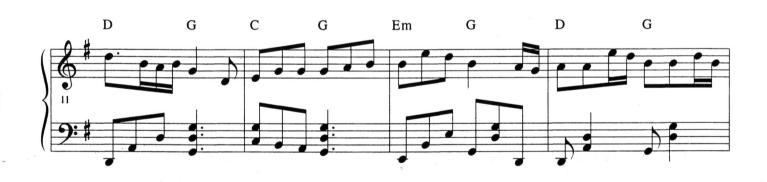

Give Me Your Hand, *Tabhair dom do Lámh,* is believed to have been composed in the 16th century by Ruaidhí Dall 'O Catháin. The story goes that Ruaidhí spent most of his time in Scotland and that he was a man of wealth himself. He appeared on day at the door of a neighbor, a Madame Ellington, who treated him far below the level of respect that he was accustomed to. When she discovered that he was a rich and famous harper, she ran to apologize, and this tune, *Tabhair dom do Lámh, (Give Me Your Hand),* was composed by Ruaidhí to show that there were no hard feelings. The moral of the story is **always treat people with respect.** They might turn out to be an Irish harper!

The Last Rose of Summer

Trad. melody with text by Thomas Moore (1779-1852)
Arr. Dennis Doyle
© 1995

Londonderry Air

Trad. Irish
Arr. Dennis Doyle and Mark Romano
© 1993

28

Londonderry Air is known by most people as **Danny Boy**, but that title and text are only the most recent reincarnation of this melody which was believed to have been composed in the 16th century. The modern words, *Oh, Danny Boy, the pipes are calling...* are only about 100 years old. A much earlier version, translated from the Irish, goes like this: *Would God I were a little apple, or one of the small daisies, or a rose in the garden, where thou art accustomed to walk alone...* and so on. There are a least five published versions of words set to this famous melody.

The Minstrel Boy

Trad. melody with text by Thomas Moore (1779-1852)
Arr. Dennis Doyle
© 1995

Broadly and spritely as a march

Thomas Moore took the music for *The Minstrel Boy* from the air *The Moreen.*

The text is as follows:

The Minstrel Boy to the war is gone,
In the ranks of death you'll find him;
His father's sword he hath girded on,
And his wild harp slung behind him;
"Land of Song!" cried the warrior bard,
"Tho' all the world betrays thee,
One sword, at least, thy rights shall guard,
One faithful harp shall praise thee!"

The Minstrel fell! But the foeman's steel
Could not bring that proud soul under;
The harp he lov'd ne'er spoke again,
For he tore its chords asunder;
And said,"No chains shall sully thee,
Thou soul of love and brav'ry!
Thy songs were made for the pure and free
They shall never sound in slavery!"

Miss Goulding

Trad. Irish attributed to Turlough O'Carolan (1670-1738)
Arr. Dennis Doyle
© 1995

The New Land

Trad. Irish Air, *An t-Oileán Ur*
Arr. Dennis Doyle
© 1995

A Night in Bethlehem

Trad. Irish, *Don Oíche Úd I mBeithil*
Arr. Dennis Doyle
© 1989

33

Oft in the Stilly Night

Arr. Dennis Doyle
© 1993

Slow and stately

Harp

The Parting Glass

Trad. Irish Air
Arr. Dennis Doyle
© 1995

35

My personal wish for the world, Siochán

Peace

Dennis Doyle
© 1990

Planxty Safaigh

Trad. Irish attributed to Turlough O'Carolan (1670-1738)
Arr. Dennis Doyle
© 1995

37

Planxty Wilkenson

Trad. Irish, attributed to Turlough O'Carolan
Arr. Dennis Doyle and Mark Romano
© 1988

Planxty Wilkenson is a piece by Carolan. It is believed that Wilkenson was a man of property who lived near the ancient Hill of Tara.

The Rakes of Mallow

Trad. Irish Reel
Arr. Dennis Doyle
© 1995

The Rights of Man (and Woman)

Traditional Irish hornpipe named after the work of Thomas Paine.
Arr. Dennis Doyle
© 1995

Róisín Dubh

Trad. Irish Air, *My Dark Rosaleen*
Arr. Dennis Doyle
© 1995

Freely, as in sean nós singing

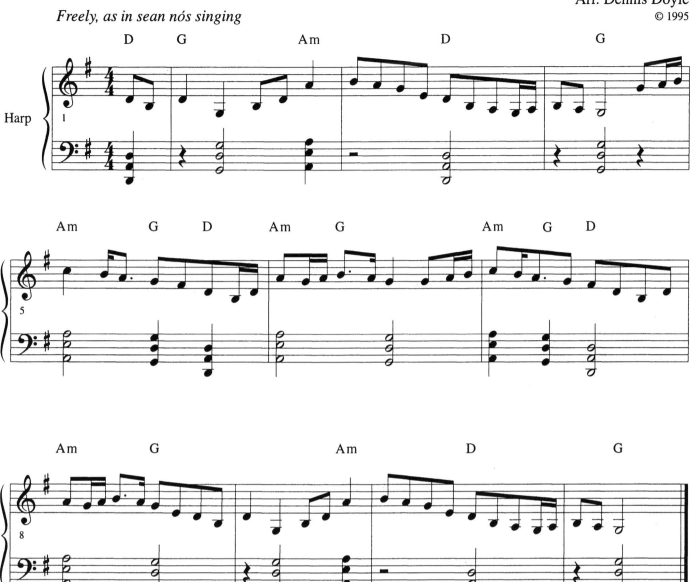

Is Trua Gan Peata

Trad. Irish song, *'Tis a Pity I'm Without My Pet*
Arr. Dennis Doyle
© 1995

The Yellow Bittern

Trad. Irish song, *An Bunnan Bui*
Arr. Dennis Doyle
© 1988

The Fairy Queen

Part A & B

Carolan
Arr. Dennis Doyle
© 1995

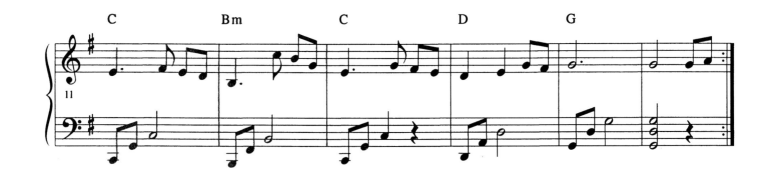

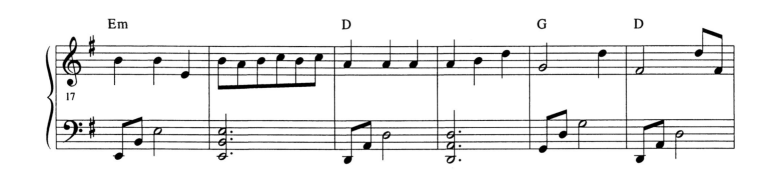

Carolan's Quarrel with the Landlady

Attr. to Turlough O'Carolan
Arr. Dennis Doyle
© 1995

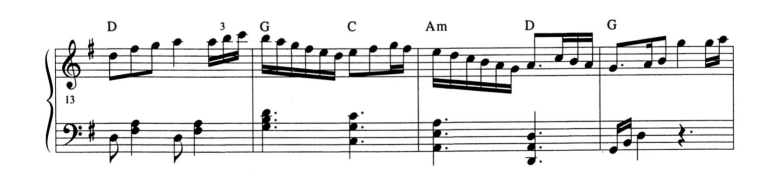

Great Music at Your Fingertips